From Pixels to Reality:
The Evolution of Virtual Reality

By

Winnie D. Diehl

TABLE OF CONTENTS

CHAPTER I
Introduction..5
   A. The birth of virtual reality (VR)...5
     The Early Days of VR Technology:...5
     Pioneering Efforts and Early Applications:...6
   B. The allure and potential of VR...9
     Virtual Experiences and Escapism:..9
     Promises of Immersive Entertainment and Education:.......................... 11

CHAPTER II
The Foundations of Virtual Reality... 14
   A. Understanding the Technology:...14
     The Components of VR Systems:..14
     Graphics, Rendering, and Resolution Advancements:........................... 16
   B. The Role of Human-Computer Interaction:... 18
     Input Devices and Haptic Feedback:... 19
     User Interface Design for VR Experiences:... 21

CHAPTER III
Virtual Reality in Entertainment.. 23
   A. Gaming and the Rise of VR:...23
     Early VR Gaming Experiments:... 23
     Impact on the Gaming Industry:...25
   B. Storytelling and Cinematic Experiences:..28
     VR Films and Storytelling Techniques:... 28
     Blurring the Lines Between Traditional and VR Narratives:......................30

CHAPTER IV
Virtual Reality in Education and Training.. 33
   A. Immersive Learning Environments:..33
     VR in Classrooms and Educational Settings:.. 33
     Skills Training and Simulations:... 35
   B. Virtual Reality for Professional Development:.. 37
     Corporate Training and Skill Enhancement:.. 38
     The Benefits and Challenges of VR Integration:.....................................39

CHAPTER V
Virtual Reality in Healthcare and Therapy...43
   A. VR for Medical Training and Practice:..43
     Surgical Simulations and Medical Education:... 43
     Advancements in Patient Care through VR:...45
   B. Therapeutic Applications of Virtual Reality:...48
     Mental Health Treatment and Exposure Therapy:...................................48
     Rehabilitation and Physical Therapy:..50

CHAPTER VI
Ethical and Social Considerations of VR..**53**
    A. Addressing VR Addiction and Mental Health Risks:...53
        Psychological Impact and Addiction Potential:..53
        Balancing Virtual Experiences with Real-World Interactions:........................55
    B. Privacy and Security in Virtual Environments:...57
        Data Protection and User Privacy Concerns:...58
        Ethical Implications of Virtual Interactions and Identity:.................................59

CHAPTER VII
The Future of Virtual Reality...**63**
    A. Emerging Technologies and Possibilities:...63
        Augmented Reality and Mixed Reality Developments:...................................63
        VR Innovations Beyond Visual and Auditory Experiences:.............................65
    B. Integrating VR into Society:..68
        VR's Potential Impact on Various Industries:...68
        Anticipated Challenges and the Road Ahead:...70

Conclusion..**73**
    A. Reflections on the Journey:..73
    B. The Transformative Power of VR:...76
    C. Looking Forward: The Next Frontier of Virtual Reality....................................80

CHAPTER I
Introduction

A. The birth of virtual reality (VR)

Virtual Reality (VR) - a term that has captured the imaginations of millions, promising an escape from reality and the advent of a new era in human-computer interaction. In this technological age, where pixels and code intertwine to create mesmerizing digital landscapes, VR stands at the forefront of innovation, offering a portal to alternative worlds and experiences. This journey from pixels to reality has been an exhilarating one, spanning several decades and characterized by a relentless pursuit of bridging the gap between the physical and digital realms.

The Early Days of VR Technology:

The roots of VR can be traced back to the mid-20th century, where curious minds began to explore the possibilities of computer-generated simulations. In the 1950s, cinematographer Morton Heilig introduced the Sensorama, an immersive theater experience that tantalized audiences with stereoscopic 3D visuals, surround sound, vibrations, and even scents. This pioneering creation laid the foundation for what would later become VR technology.

In the 1960s, computer scientist Ivan Sutherland made a groundbreaking contribution to the field with the invention of the "Sword of Damocles." This bulky and cumbersome device, suspended from the ceiling, featured a head-mounted display (HMD) connected to a computer. Despite its limitations, the "Sword of Damocles" was a pivotal step forward, offering users a glimpse into computer-generated virtual environments.

Pioneering Efforts and Early Applications:

The 1980s witnessed a surge of interest in VR, as computing power improved, and innovative minds sought to push the boundaries further. Notable efforts like Jaron Lanier's "Virtual Reality" company and the development of the DataGlove by Thomas Zimmerman and Jaron Lanier himself were crucial milestones during this period. The DataGlove allowed users to interact with virtual objects, enhancing the sense of immersion and opening doors to a myriad of potential applications.

Despite the progress, VR technology faced significant challenges during its early days, particularly in terms of hardware limitations and high costs. However, this did not deter pioneers, as they recognized the immense potential of VR in various domains. Aerospace and military industries were among the first to adopt VR for flight simulation and training purposes, capitalizing on the ability to recreate real-life scenarios in safe and controlled environments.

The entertainment sector also saw the allure of VR, experimenting with arcade-style setups that transported players into digital worlds. Though crude by today's standards, these early gaming experiences laid the groundwork for the revolution to come.

As the years progressed, research and development in the field intensified, leading to the birth of VR headsets like the Virtuality series in the early 1990s. Despite offering a more refined VR experience, consumer interest remained relatively modest due to high costs and a limited selection of content.

Nonetheless, these pioneering efforts laid a crucial foundation for the future of VR, demonstrating that the concept was not just a fleeting fad but a technology with vast potential waiting to be unlocked. The journey from the early days of VR to the sophisticated systems we have today has been marked by determination, ingenuity, and an unyielding belief in the power of virtual reality to revolutionize how we interact with digital content and each other.

In the subsequent sections of this book, we will delve deeper into the evolution of VR, exploring its applications in entertainment, education, healthcare, and beyond. We will also confront the ethical and social considerations surrounding this transformative technology and peer into the future, where VR's journey is poised to continue, fueled by the ever-accelerating advancements in computing, graphics, and human imagination.

B. The allure and potential of VR

In the realm of technology, where innovation unfolds at an astounding pace, Virtual Reality (VR) has emerged as a beacon of wonder, promising to revolutionize how we perceive and interact with the digital world. As we journey from pixels to reality, VR stands as a transformative force, blurring the lines between the physical and the virtual, captivating minds and hearts alike. In this introduction, we will explore the allure and boundless potential that VR holds, captivating our senses with virtual experiences, offering an escape from the mundane, and unlocking new frontiers in entertainment and education.

Virtual Experiences and Escapism:

At the heart of VR's allure lies the promise of transcending reality, transporting ourselves into alternate dimensions, and living through experiences that defy the constraints of the physical world. Whether it's exploring fantastical landscapes, delving into historical epochs, or venturing into uncharted territories, VR bestows upon us the gift of immersion like never before.

With a VR headset adorning our eyes and the world around us fading into oblivion, we become the architects of our reality. We can traverse the depths of the ocean, touch the stars in distant galaxies, or stand on the edge of a virtual skyscraper, feeling our hearts race with an intoxicating blend of thrill and trepidation. VR turns dreams into palpable realities, fostering a profound connection between our minds and the virtual realms we inhabit.

Moreover, VR offers an enticing avenue for escapism, providing respite from the stress and monotony of everyday life. When the weight of the world becomes overwhelming, we can don a VR headset and escape to tranquil paradises, embark on grand adventures, or simply unwind in soothing virtual environments. The therapeutic potential of VR for stress relief and mental well-being has garnered significant attention, presenting a path to cultivate mindfulness and serenity amidst the chaos of modern living.

Promises of Immersive Entertainment and Education:

The realm of entertainment has witnessed a seismic shift with the advent of VR. No longer confined to passive observation, we are now active participants in narratives that unfold around us. VR gaming, in particular, has emerged as a trailblazer, elevating gameplay to exhilarating heights. As we wield virtual weapons, cast spells, or solve enigmatic puzzles, we are drawn deeper into the virtual fabric, where our actions carry tangible consequences. This unprecedented level of engagement and agency fosters an emotional bond between players and their virtual personas, making the gaming experience profoundly personal and unforgettable.

Beyond gaming, VR has seeped into other facets of entertainment, including immersive storytelling through VR films and virtual concerts that teleport audiences to front-row seats with their favorite artists. As content creators continue to push the boundaries of creativity, the possibilities for VR-driven entertainment seem boundless.

Education, too, stands to be revolutionized by the vast potential of VR. Traditional classrooms can be transformed into interactive and dynamic learning environments, where students engage directly with historical events, scientific concepts, and cultural wonders. Instead of reading about the ancient pyramids of Egypt, students can virtually stand amid the towering structures, basking in the grandeur of history. Complex scientific theories can be brought to life through interactive simulations, making learning a captivating and immersive journey of discovery.

Moreover, VR enables experiential learning, allowing individuals to practice skills and professions in safe and controlled virtual spaces. From medical students performing intricate surgeries to astronauts undergoing extraterrestrial training, the practical applications of VR in education are limited only by our imagination.

In conclusion, the allure of Virtual Reality lies in its potential to redefine our reality and liberate our imaginations. With the ability to whisk us away to far-off lands, facilitate transformative entertainment experiences, and revolutionize how we learn, VR stands as a testament to the ingenuity of human endeavor. As we embark on this exploration of VR's evolution, we will delve deeper into the foundations of this technology, its applications across various industries, and the ethical considerations that accompany its extraordinary rise to prominence. The pixels that once seemed distant and detached from reality are now converging, beckoning us to embrace a future where the virtual and the real intertwine in harmonious synergy.

CHAPTER II
The Foundations of Virtual Reality

A. Understanding the Technology:

Virtual Reality (VR) is not a single entity but a complex amalgamation of cutting-edge technologies working in unison to create a seamless and immersive experience for users. To comprehend the magic behind VR, we must delve into the intricacies of its underlying foundations.

The Components of VR Systems:

At the core of any VR system lie several vital components, each playing a crucial role in shaping the virtual experience. The VR headset, perhaps the most recognizable element, is the gateway that connects users to the virtual realm. Equipped with high-resolution displays, these headsets render the digital world before our eyes. Additionally, modern headsets often incorporate position tracking sensors, enabling precise tracking of head movements to synchronize the virtual perspective with the user's real-world orientation.

Hand controllers or motion-tracking devices are another integral part of VR systems. These controllers enable users to interact with the virtual environment, bringing a sense of realism and agency to the experience. Whether grabbing objects, pointing, or gesturing, these controllers bridge the gap between our physical actions and their digital counterparts.

Behind the scenes, a powerful computer or gaming console acts as the engine that drives the VR experience. These computing powerhouses process vast amounts of data in real-time, ensuring that the virtual world responds instantaneously to our interactions. To maintain seamless performance and prevent motion sickness, VR systems require robust graphics processing units (GPUs) and central processing units (CPUs) capable of handling the computational demands.

Furthermore, audio plays an integral role in creating a convincing and immersive environment. Spatial sound technologies envelop users in a 3D soundscape, where sounds emanate from their virtual locations, enhancing the overall sense of presence and immersion.

Graphics, Rendering, and Resolution Advancements:

One of the critical challenges in VR development is achieving realistic and visually stunning graphics that suspend disbelief. In the early days of VR, hardware limitations often led to pixelated and rudimentary visuals. However, rapid advancements in graphics technology have transformed VR into a realm of unparalleled visual fidelity.

Real-time rendering, where the virtual environment is generated on the fly as the user explores it, is the cornerstone of modern VR graphics. Rendering engines utilize sophisticated algorithms and shading techniques to simulate lighting, shadows, and textures, resulting in lifelike environments that respond naturally to changing light conditions.

Resolution is a vital aspect of VR visuals. Higher resolution displays ensure that the virtual world appears sharp and detailed, reducing the dreaded "screen door effect" where visible gaps between pixels hinder immersion. Advancements in display technologies, such as OLED and LCD panels, have enabled VR headsets to achieve impressive resolutions, minimizing visual artifacts and maximizing the sense of presence.

To enhance realism further, VR developers are exploring the potential of ray tracing technology. Ray tracing simulates the behavior of light rays in the virtual environment, resulting in stunningly realistic reflections, refractions, and shadows. By incorporating ray tracing into VR rendering pipelines, developers can elevate the visual quality to new heights, drawing users deeper into the virtual worlds they inhabit.

While graphics and rendering advancements are crucial, developers also face the challenge of optimizing performance to maintain smooth and consistent frame rates. A lag or stutter in VR can break the sense of immersion and lead to discomfort. Hence, developers employ techniques like foveated rendering, which prioritizes rendering fidelity in the user's immediate field of view, while reducing detail in peripheral areas where visual acuity is lower.

In conclusion, the foundations of VR technology encompass an intricate interplay of hardware and software innovations. From the components of VR systems that immerse us in the experience to the remarkable strides in graphics, rendering, and resolution, each aspect contributes to creating a realm where the boundary between reality and virtuality blurs. As we continue our exploration of VR's evolution, we will delve into its applications in entertainment, education, healthcare, and other domains, witnessing how these technological foundations have paved the way for a new era of human interaction with digital realms.

B. The Role of Human-Computer Interaction:

As Virtual Reality (VR) evolves into a compelling medium that entices our senses and sparks our imaginations, the crucial aspect that bridges the gap between the user and the virtual world is Human-Computer Interaction (HCI). This intricate interplay between humans and machines is a key determinant of the level of immersion, comfort, and usability that VR experiences can achieve. In this section, we will explore the pivotal role of HCI in VR, focusing on input devices and haptic feedback as well as the significance of user interface design to craft seamless and intuitive virtual experiences.

Input Devices and Haptic Feedback:

VR's magic lies in its capacity to let users engage with digital environments in ways that simulate real-world interactions. Input devices play a pivotal role in this regard, translating our physical movements and actions into corresponding actions within the virtual realm.

Motion controllers are a fundamental part of the VR interaction ecosystem. These handheld devices are equipped with various sensors, such as accelerometers and gyroscopes, to precisely track their positions and orientations in 3D space. As users wield these controllers, they can interact with virtual objects, pick up items, manipulate elements, and engage in gestures that mirror their real-life counterparts.

Beyond motion controllers, VR also explores novel input methods, such as hand and finger tracking. With the integration of sophisticated cameras and machine learning algorithms, VR systems can discern and interpret the intricate movements of users' hands and fingers. This direct interaction without the need for controllers enhances the sense of immersion and intuitiveness.

Another crucial aspect of HCI in VR is haptic feedback. Haptic feedback involves providing users with tactile sensations to simulate the sense of touch. VR developers employ various techniques, such as vibrating controllers or force-feedback gloves, to convey different textures, pressures, and interactions with virtual objects. Haptic feedback is instrumental in making VR experiences more realistic and engaging, enabling users to feel a sense of presence and physicality in the digital environment.

User Interface Design for VR Experiences:

User Interface (UI) design is a cornerstone of VR experiences, as it dictates how users navigate, interact, and comprehend the virtual environment. In VR, UI design is particularly challenging, as traditional flat-screen interfaces are inadequate for the immersive 3D environment that surrounds users.

One of the key principles in VR UI design is to minimize clutter and distractions. Developers strive to create intuitive and straightforward interfaces that seamlessly integrate into the virtual world without overshadowing the immersive experience. This involves crafting menus, buttons, and information displays that are easily accessible and non-intrusive, allowing users to focus on the VR content itself.

A critical consideration in VR UI design is user comfort and ergonomics. Since VR is a fully immersive experience, prolonged usage can lead to fatigue and motion sickness. Designers must carefully position UI elements, avoid sudden movements, and provide ergonomic solutions for interactions to ensure user comfort and well-being.

Furthermore, developers explore innovative UI paradigms that leverage VR's spatial capabilities. For instance, volumetric menus that float in the virtual space around the user, or gesture-based interactions that mimic real-world gestures, are becoming increasingly prevalent. These design choices enhance the sense of immersion and encourage a more natural and intuitive user experience. To cater to diverse audiences, VR experiences must also consider accessibility in UI design. Ensuring that the VR environment is accessible to users with disabilities or limited physical abilities involves thoughtful implementation of alternative interaction methods and UI elements that accommodate a wide range of users.

In conclusion, HCI stands as a linchpin that elevates VR experiences from being mere spectacles to immersive and interactive realms. Input devices and haptic feedback empower users to wield agency in the virtual environment, while thoughtful UI design crafts interfaces that integrate seamlessly into the VR world.

CHAPTER III
Virtual Reality in Entertainment

A. Gaming and the Rise of VR:

Within the vast realm of Virtual Reality (VR), gaming stands as one of its most captivating and transformative applications. From the early experiments to the modern-day innovations, VR gaming has become a driving force that redefines the landscape of interactive entertainment. In this section, we will explore the fascinating journey of VR gaming, from its humble beginnings as experimental prototypes to its significant impact on the gaming industry.

Early VR Gaming Experiments:

The concept of VR gaming has intrigued visionaries and game developers for decades, even before the technology had matured to bring these dreams to life. During the 1980s and 1990s, visionary pioneers like Jaron Lanier and his "Virtual Reality" company, along with other trailblazers, laid the groundwork for what was to come. However, the hardware limitations and the nascent state of VR technology hindered widespread adoption and relegated VR gaming to the realm of science fiction.

It wasn't until the mid-2010s that VR gaming made a significant resurgence. Key players like Oculus, HTC, and Sony unveiled consumer-grade VR headsets that transformed these dreams into tangible reality. The Oculus Rift, released in 2016, and the HTC Vive, showcased the potential of immersive gaming, allowing players to step into virtual worlds and interact with them like never before.

The launch of the Oculus Rift and HTC Vive marked a turning point, igniting a frenzy of interest in VR gaming and inspiring developers to create experiences that pushed the boundaries of creativity and innovation. Early VR gaming experiences were a mix of awe-inspiring wonders and experimental concepts, as developers tested the waters to discover what worked best in this new medium.

Impact on the Gaming Industry:

The resurgence of VR gaming sparked a wave of excitement and anticipation among gamers and developers alike. The gaming industry, always on the lookout for transformative technologies, quickly recognized the potential of VR to revolutionize the gaming experience. The impact of VR on the gaming industry has been multifaceted, reshaping various aspects of game development and consumption.

a. Immersion and Empathy: VR gaming's most potent asset is its unparalleled sense of immersion. As players don the VR headset and enter virtual worlds, they find themselves at the center of the action, no longer observers but active participants. This heightened level of immersion fosters a sense of empathy, as players feel emotionally connected to the virtual characters and environments. The result is an emotional investment in the gaming experience that traditional gaming mediums could not achieve.

b. Innovation and Novel Gameplay: VR opens up new frontiers for game design and mechanics. Developers have explored innovative gameplay mechanics, such as using hand gestures for spellcasting, physically ducking behind cover to evade enemy fire, or solving puzzles by manipulating virtual objects. These novel gameplay elements breathe new life into established genres and spark creativity that reverberates throughout the gaming industry.

c. Expanding Horizons for Game Developers: VR gaming presents both opportunities and challenges for game developers. While creating VR experiences requires specialized knowledge and a different approach to design, it also allows developers to explore uncharted territories and deliver unique experiences. Independent developers, in particular, have embraced VR as a platform to showcase their creativity, resulting in an influx of diverse and experimental VR titles.

d. A Catalyst for Technological Advancement: The demand for VR gaming experiences has driven significant advancements in hardware and software technologies. GPU manufacturers have released powerful graphics cards tailored for VR, and innovations like eye-tracking and foveated rendering aim to optimize performance and enhance visual fidelity. These advancements not only benefit VR gaming but also spill over into other applications of VR.

e. Building Communities and Social VR: VR gaming has facilitated the growth of vibrant communities where players can meet, socialize, and share experiences in virtual spaces. Social VR platforms allow users to interact with friends and strangers in immersive environments, fostering a new era of connectedness and shared adventures.

In conclusion, VR gaming has come a long way from its early experiments to its current position as a transformative force in the entertainment industry. With its ability to immerse players in captivating virtual worlds and redefine gaming experiences, VR has left an indelible mark on the gaming landscape. As the technology continues to evolve and more developers push the boundaries of creativity, VR gaming's impact is poised to shape the future of interactive entertainment, blurring the lines between the real and the virtual with every immersive step.

B. Storytelling and Cinematic Experiences:

As Virtual Reality (VR) evolves into a captivating medium, it becomes a potent canvas for storytelling, ushering in a new era of immersive cinematic experiences. The boundaries between traditional filmmaking and VR narratives blur as creators harness the power of this transformative technology to craft compelling stories that transcend the limits of the screen. In this section, we will explore the emergence of VR films and the storytelling techniques that breathe life into these captivating virtual narratives, as well as the profound impact they have on the art of storytelling.

VR Films and Storytelling Techniques:

VR films, also known as cinematic VR experiences, transport audiences from the passive role of spectators to active participants within the narrative. Unlike traditional films, where the camera's perspective dictates what viewers see, VR films empower users to explore the story at their own pace, enabling a personalized and interactive narrative experience.

The art of VR storytelling requires a fundamental shift in how directors, writers, and filmmakers approach their craft. Instead of merely framing shots, they must create entire virtual worlds where the story unfolds in a way that captures the viewer's attention from all angles. This entails constructing detailed environments that immerse audiences, captivating their senses and emotions.

One of the core storytelling techniques in VR films is the use of spatial audio. Spatial audio enables sound to emanate from specific locations within the virtual world, providing a sense of presence and directionality. This technique complements the visual experience, ensuring that audio cues lead viewers' attention to critical plot points, characters, or scenic elements.

Moreover, storytelling in VR often incorporates branching narratives and interactive elements. Viewers can make choices that affect the progression of the story, leading to different outcomes and personalized experiences. This interactivity fosters a sense of agency, allowing viewers to feel deeply engaged and emotionally invested in the characters and their fate.

Another key technique is the use of visual cues and subtle directing to guide viewers' attention. While traditional films rely on editing and camera movement to direct the audience's focus, VR directors must guide attention through spatial composition and the placement of narrative elements within the 3D environment. Viewers are encouraged to explore the scenes, discovering essential details that contribute to the overall narrative.

Blurring the Lines Between Traditional and VR Narratives:

VR storytelling does not seek to replace traditional filmmaking but instead enriches it by offering a complementary and unique form of expression. As VR films blur the lines between the real and the virtual, they create a profound sense of presence and emotional connection that traditional films may struggle to achieve.

A fascinating trend is the convergence of traditional filmmaking techniques with VR narratives. Filmmakers are experimenting with techniques like "360-degree filmmaking," where they capture scenes from multiple angles simultaneously, akin to placing the viewer within the heart of the action. This approach blends the art of traditional filmmaking with the immersive potential of VR, resulting in breathtaking and emotionally charged experiences.

Moreover, VR narratives have inspired filmmakers to explore nonlinear storytelling and new narrative structures. In traditional linear storytelling, the plot unfolds in a fixed sequence, while VR narratives can be nonlinear, allowing viewers to explore the story's various facets at their pace. This freedom to explore and discover encourages repeated viewings, uncovering new layers of meaning with each interaction.

The collaborative nature of VR filmmaking is another aspect that blurs the lines between traditional and VR narratives. In VR, directors and creators work closely with programmers, 3D artists, sound designers, and other specialists to bring the virtual world to life. This collaborative approach is akin to the traditional film production process, fostering an atmosphere of creativity and innovation.

In conclusion, VR storytelling marks a profound shift in the art of entertainment, inviting audiences into immersive cinematic experiences like never before. With innovative techniques that leverage spatial audio, interactivity, and branching narratives, VR films empower viewers to be active participants in the story, forging emotional connections with characters and settings. As VR and traditional filmmaking converge, storytellers are reimagining the boundaries of narrative expression, giving rise to a new era of captivating and emotionally resonant entertainment that thrives in the boundless realms of Virtual Reality.

CHAPTER IV
Virtual Reality in Education and Training

A. Immersive Learning Environments:

Virtual Reality (VR) has emerged as a transformative tool in the field of education and training, revolutionizing how knowledge is imparted and skills are honed. By creating immersive learning environments, VR opens new frontiers of experiential education that engage learners like never before. In this section, we will explore the integration of VR in classrooms and educational settings, as well as its use in skills training and simulations, revolutionizing the way we learn and prepare for real-world challenges.

VR in Classrooms and Educational Settings:

Traditional classrooms have long been the bedrock of formal education, but VR is now augmenting these spaces with immersive learning experiences. As students don VR headsets, they are transported to historical events, foreign countries, or even microscopic realms that are otherwise inaccessible in the physical world. This firsthand exposure enriches their understanding of subjects and fosters a deep sense of curiosity and engagement.

In history classes, VR can recreate iconic moments, allowing students to witness events like the signing of the Declaration of Independence or the moon landing, as if they were present in the past. In geography, students can traverse global landscapes, exploring diverse ecosystems and understanding the impact of climate change in real time.

Furthermore, VR unlocks the potential for experiential learning. Instead of reading about scientific concepts, students can now conduct virtual experiments and observe the outcomes, encouraging a deeper grasp of scientific principles. Subjects like anatomy and biology become interactive journeys, where students can virtually explore the human body and its intricacies.

Moreover, VR fosters inclusivity by accommodating different learning styles and abilities. It offers diverse modes of interaction, catering to both visual and kinesthetic learners. Additionally, learners with physical or cognitive challenges can participate in virtual classrooms with ease, as the virtual environment provides flexible and accessible learning opportunities.

Skills Training and Simulations:

Beyond the traditional classroom, VR has become a powerful tool for skills training across various industries. Simulations in VR enable trainees to practice and refine skills in safe and controlled environments, reducing the risks associated with real-world training.

In healthcare, VR simulations allow medical students to perform virtual surgeries, honing their surgical techniques and decision-making without endangering patients. These realistic simulations enhance the competence and confidence of future healthcare professionals, equipping them with vital experience before they step into an operating room.

In the realm of aviation, VR plays a critical role in pilot training. Aspiring pilots can practice flying in various weather conditions, facing challenging scenarios, and responding to emergencies, all within a risk-free virtual environment. This results in better-prepared pilots who can handle complex situations with composure and precision.

Similarly, the military utilizes VR for tactical training and mission rehearsals. Soldiers can immerse themselves in realistic combat scenarios, preparing for the complexities of the battlefield without exposing themselves to physical harm.

VR is also revolutionizing training in industries like manufacturing, engineering, and emergency response. Employees can practice using specialized equipment, troubleshoot potential issues, and familiarize themselves with complex processes before entering the actual workspace.

The gamification of training through VR adds an element of fun and engagement, motivating trainees to actively participate and master new skills. By providing immediate feedback and performance analytics, VR training enables learners to track their progress and identify areas for improvement, leading to more efficient skill acquisition.

In conclusion, VR's foray into education and training brings forth immersive learning environments that transcend the traditional boundaries of teaching and instruction. As VR integrates into classrooms, students are empowered with experiential learning that captivates their minds and fuels their curiosity. In the realm of skills training and simulations, VR revolutionizes how professionals acquire and refine competencies, preparing them for real-world challenges with unprecedented confidence. As technology continues to advance, the possibilities for VR in education and training are limitless, heralding a future where immersive learning becomes an indispensable aspect of personal and professional development.

B. Virtual Reality for Professional Development:

Virtual Reality (VR) has emerged as a game-changer in the realm of professional development, offering an immersive and effective platform for corporate training and skill enhancement. As businesses and organizations seek innovative ways to empower their workforce, VR integration in professional development has proven to be a transformative approach. In this section, we will explore the application of VR in corporate training and skill enhancement, as well as the myriad benefits it brings and the challenges that come with its integration.

Corporate Training and Skill Enhancement:

Traditional methods of corporate training often involve classroom sessions or online modules, but VR takes learning to new heights by providing realistic and hands-on experiences. With VR, employees can participate in interactive and scenario-based training that simulates real-life situations, preparing them for on-the-job challenges.

In the realm of sales and customer service, VR enables employees to engage in simulated customer interactions, where they can practice handling various scenarios and refining their communication skills. This fosters a higher level of confidence and competence when dealing with actual customers, leading to improved customer satisfaction and retention.

For leadership and management training, VR offers a safe environment for honing decision-making and conflict resolution skills. Managers can navigate complex interpersonal dynamics and practice handling difficult conversations, gaining valuable experience that translates into more effective leadership.

VR is also transforming technical and hands-on training. Whether it's in manufacturing, engineering, or maintenance, employees can learn to operate machinery, troubleshoot equipment, or assemble products within a virtual setting. This not only reduces the risk of accidents during training but also streamlines the learning process, as trainees can repeat tasks until they achieve proficiency.

The Benefits and Challenges of VR Integration:

a. Benefits of VR Integration:

i. Realistic Simulations: VR provides authentic and lifelike simulations, enabling learners to experience scenarios that closely mirror real-world situations. This heightened sense of realism enhances the transfer of knowledge and skills to actual job settings.

ii. Active Learning and Engagement: VR's interactive nature fosters active learning, as participants must engage with the environment and make decisions in real-time. This active engagement leads to deeper understanding and retention of information.

iii. Personalized Learning Paths: VR training can adapt to individual learner needs, allowing employees to progress at their pace and focus on areas that require improvement. This personalized approach maximizes the effectiveness of training.

iv. Cost-Effectiveness: While the initial investment in VR technology may be substantial, long-term benefits include reduced training costs due to the elimination of physical training spaces, equipment, and travel expenses.

v. Scalability: Once developed, VR training modules can be easily scaled to accommodate a large number of learners across different locations. This scalability makes it an ideal solution for companies with a distributed workforce.

b. Challenges of VR Integration:

i. Cost and Accessibility: High-quality VR hardware and software can be expensive, making initial implementation a significant investment for organizations. Additionally, ensuring accessibility for all employees may be challenging, especially for those in remote locations.

ii. Content Development: Creating effective VR training content requires specialized expertise and resources. Developing high-quality, interactive simulations can be time-consuming and costly.

iii. Technical Issues: VR systems may encounter technical glitches or compatibility issues, which can disrupt the training experience. Organizations need robust technical support and maintenance to ensure smooth training sessions.

iv. Learning Curve: Some employees may find it challenging to adapt to VR technology initially, leading to a learning curve that could impact the effectiveness of training.

v. Ethical Considerations: VR simulations designed to replicate challenging situations must be developed with sensitivity and ethical considerations, ensuring that the training does not cause distress or harm to participants.

Virtual Reality's integration into professional development represents a paradigm shift in corporate training and skill enhancement. By providing immersive and lifelike simulations, VR empowers employees to learn and practice in safe and engaging environments, fostering competence and confidence. The benefits of VR integration, such as realistic simulations, active learning, and scalability, promise to revolutionize the way businesses invest in the growth and development of their workforce. Despite challenges related to cost, accessibility, and content development, the potential for VR to transform professional development is immense.

CHAPTER V
Virtual Reality in Healthcare and Therapy

A. VR for Medical Training and Practice:

Virtual Reality (VR) has found a remarkable application in the realm of healthcare and therapy, revolutionizing medical training and patient care. As technology continues to evolve, VR's impact on medical education and practice becomes increasingly profound, providing immersive simulations and advancements that enhance patient outcomes. In this section, we will explore the use of VR in surgical simulations and medical education, as well as the remarkable advancements in patient care that VR brings to the forefront.

Surgical Simulations and Medical Education:

Surgical training is a critical aspect of medical education, where precision and experience are paramount. VR has emerged as a game-changing tool in surgical simulations, allowing medical students and surgeons to practice complex procedures in a risk-free virtual environment.

Virtual surgical simulations offer a realistic representation of the human anatomy, allowing trainees to interact with virtual organs, tissues, and structures. As they manipulate virtual instruments, VR provides haptic feedback, simulating the resistance and response that one would encounter during actual surgery. This hands-on experience refines surgical skills, leading to improved dexterity and proficiency.

For aspiring surgeons, VR can be instrumental in building confidence before they perform procedures on live patients. By providing a platform to rehearse surgeries repeatedly, VR minimizes the potential for errors and complications, ultimately leading to better patient outcomes.

Medical students can also benefit from VR-based anatomy lessons. Instead of relying solely on textbooks and cadaver dissections, VR allows students to explore 3D models of organs and systems, facilitating a deeper understanding of human anatomy. This visual and interactive learning experience enhances medical education and promotes a more comprehensive grasp of complex anatomical structures.

Advancements in Patient Care through VR:

VR's influence in patient care extends beyond medical education to directly impact the treatment and well-being of patients.

a. Pain Management: VR has shown promise as a non-pharmacological intervention for pain management. By immersing patients in calming and distracting virtual environments, VR reduces the perception of pain and discomfort. For patients undergoing painful procedures or those dealing with chronic pain, VR provides a welcome respite, enhancing their overall experience.

b. Therapy and Rehabilitation: VR-based therapies have gained traction in various rehabilitation programs. Patients recovering from physical injuries or neurological conditions can engage in virtual exercises and activities tailored to their specific needs. These therapeutic interventions promote motor skills, cognitive function, and emotional well-being.

c. Exposure Therapy: VR has proven effective in exposure therapy for patients with phobias, anxiety disorders, or post-traumatic stress disorder (PTSD). By gradually exposing patients to triggering situations in a controlled virtual environment, therapists can help individuals confront and manage their fears, leading to reduced anxiety and improved coping mechanisms.

d. Cognitive Rehabilitation: VR provides a platform for cognitive rehabilitation programs that assist patients with cognitive impairments resulting from brain injuries or neurodegenerative disorders. These programs offer personalized challenges and exercises to improve memory, attention, and executive function.

e. Mental Health Interventions: Virtual environments can facilitate guided mindfulness exercises and relaxation techniques, aiding individuals in managing stress, anxiety, and depression. VR-based interventions provide a private and immersive space for therapeutic sessions.

Moreover, VR plays a significant role in telemedicine, enabling remote consultations and surgical collaborations. Surgeons can use VR to engage in real-time consultations with colleagues across the globe, discussing complex cases and collaborating on intricate surgical procedures. This globalization of expertise enhances patient care and expands access to specialized medical knowledge.

In conclusion, Virtual Reality's integration into healthcare and therapy is reshaping the landscape of medical education, surgical training, and patient care. Through immersive surgical simulations and anatomy lessons, VR empowers medical professionals to refine their skills and augment patient outcomes. Advancements in patient care, from pain management to cognitive rehabilitation, demonstrate the transformative potential of VR in enhancing the well-being of individuals facing various health challenges. As VR technology continues to progress, its applications in healthcare are poised to drive further innovations that will shape the future of medical practice, education, and patient-centric care.

B. Therapeutic Applications of Virtual Reality:

Virtual Reality (VR) has emerged as a powerful tool in the realm of healthcare and therapy, offering innovative and effective therapeutic applications that transform the landscape of mental health treatment, exposure therapy, rehabilitation, and physical therapy. Harnessing the potential of immersive experiences, VR provides new avenues for healing, empowerment, and recovery. In this section, we will explore the transformative impact of VR in mental health treatment and exposure therapy, as well as its instrumental role in rehabilitation and physical therapy.

Mental Health Treatment and Exposure Therapy:

Mental health treatment stands at the forefront of therapeutic applications of VR, leveraging its capacity to create immersive and controlled environments for therapeutic interventions.

a. Anxiety and Phobia Treatment: VR-based exposure therapy has revolutionized the treatment of anxiety disorders and phobias. Patients can be gradually exposed to their triggers in a virtual setting, allowing therapists to tailor the intensity and pace of exposure. This process helps individuals confront and manage their fears in a safe and controlled environment, fostering desensitization and reducing anxiety.

b. PTSD Treatment: Virtual Reality has shown remarkable promise in post-traumatic stress disorder (PTSD) treatment. Veterans and individuals who have experienced traumatic events can participate in virtual scenarios that resemble their trauma, guided by therapists. By revisiting and processing the trauma in a therapeutic setting, patients can work towards healing and emotional recovery.

c. Stress and Relaxation Interventions: VR offers immersive relaxation experiences that aid in stress reduction and mindfulness. Patients can immerse themselves in tranquil virtual environments, engaging in guided mindfulness exercises that promote relaxation and emotional well-being. These interventions empower individuals to manage stress and build resilience.

d. Social Anxiety Interventions: For individuals with social anxiety, VR provides a controlled setting to practice social interactions. Patients can engage in virtual scenarios, such as job interviews or public speaking, gradually building confidence and improving social skills in a safe environment.

Rehabilitation and Physical Therapy:

VR has transformed the landscape of rehabilitation and physical therapy, facilitating personalized and engaging interventions.

a. Physical Rehabilitation: In physical therapy, VR offers interactive exercises and activities tailored to the needs of individual patients. Whether recovering from injuries or neurological conditions, patients can engage in virtual exercises that promote motor skills, balance, and coordination. Real-time feedback allows therapists to monitor progress and adjust treatment plans accordingly.

b. Neurorehabilitation: VR plays a crucial role in neurorehabilitation for individuals with stroke, traumatic brain injuries, or neurological disorders. VR-based exercises target specific areas of impairment, promoting neuroplasticity and recovery. Through gamification and interactive tasks, patients are motivated to actively participate in their rehabilitation journey.

c. Pain Management: VR-based distractions and mindfulness interventions have demonstrated efficacy in pain management. Patients undergoing painful medical procedures or chronic pain management can benefit from immersive experiences that divert their attention and reduce the perception of pain.

d. Balance and Gait Training: For older adults or patients with balance disorders, VR offers specialized training to improve stability and gait. Virtual environments challenge patients to navigate different terrains and obstacles, promoting mobility and fall prevention.

VR's therapeutic applications extend beyond the confines of traditional therapy settings, offering remote interventions and telehealth solutions. Virtual reality enables therapists to deliver interventions to patients in their homes or remote locations, promoting accessibility and continuity of care.

The immersive nature of VR fosters a heightened sense of presence and engagement, making therapeutic experiences more enjoyable and motivating for patients. Additionally, VR interventions allow therapists to collect objective data and performance metrics, facilitating evidence-based decision-making and treatment planning.

In conclusion, Virtual Reality's therapeutic applications in healthcare and therapy have propelled the field into a new era of healing and recovery. From mental health treatment and exposure therapy, where VR empowers patients to confront and manage fears, to rehabilitation and physical therapy, where personalized and engaging interventions promote recovery and mobility, VR's impact is transformative. As technology advances and our understanding of the mind-body connection deepens, VR is poised to continue revolutionizing therapeutic interventions, inspiring hope and empowerment for individuals facing diverse health challenges.

CHAPTER VI
Ethical and Social Considerations of VR

A. Addressing VR Addiction and Mental Health Risks:

As Virtual Reality (VR) becomes an increasingly pervasive and captivating technology, society must grapple with ethical and social considerations surrounding its use. Among these concerns are the risks of VR addiction and potential impacts on mental health. While VR offers immersive and engaging experiences, its extensive use may lead to psychological challenges. In this section, we will explore the psychological impact and addiction potential of VR, as well as the importance of balancing virtual experiences with real-world interactions.

Psychological Impact and Addiction Potential:

VR's ability to transport users to captivating virtual realms creates the potential for psychological impact, both positive and negative. On one hand, VR can offer therapeutic benefits, such as exposure therapy for anxiety disorders or relaxation experiences for stress reduction. However, excessive or inappropriate use of VR may lead to adverse psychological effects.

VR's immersive nature can blur the boundaries between the virtual and real world, causing a phenomenon known as the "breakout effect." This effect occurs when users struggle to differentiate between virtual experiences and reality, leading to a dissociation from real-world responsibilities and relationships.

Moreover, VR addiction is a potential concern, especially when users prioritize virtual interactions over real-life obligations. Addiction to VR can negatively impact daily functioning, relationships, and overall well-being. Individuals may find themselves spending excessive amounts of time in virtual environments, leading to social isolation and neglect of important life activities.

Children and adolescents may be particularly vulnerable to the addictive allure of VR, as their developing brains are highly responsive to novel and immersive experiences. Parents, educators, and caregivers should monitor and regulate the use of VR in young populations to mitigate potential risks.

Balancing Virtual Experiences with Real-World Interactions:

Finding a balance between virtual experiences and real-world interactions is essential to maintaining social connectedness and well-being. While VR offers novel opportunities for communication and entertainment, it should not replace face-to-face interactions or the richness of real-life experiences.

The phenomenon of "VR socialization" poses ethical concerns when users prioritize virtual friendships and relationships over meaningful connections in the physical world. Maintaining genuine human connections and social bonds is critical for emotional health and social development.

To address these ethical considerations, developers and platform providers should implement measures to encourage responsible VR usage. This may include built-in reminders to take breaks, time limits on VR sessions, and notifications to encourage users to engage in real-world activities.

Educational institutions can play a role in fostering digital literacy and responsible VR usage among students. Teaching young learners about the potential risks of excessive VR consumption and the importance of balanced media engagement can empower them to make informed choices.

Furthermore, mental health professionals should be vigilant about potential VR addiction or negative psychological impacts in individuals who use VR extensively. Assessing patients' VR usage habits and addressing any adverse effects is crucial to promoting mental well-being.

As VR technology continues to advance, researchers should conduct long-term studies to investigate the potential effects of prolonged VR exposure on mental health and well-being. This research will aid in formulating evidence-based guidelines for responsible VR usage.

In conclusion, the widespread adoption of Virtual Reality brings with it ethical and social considerations that require thoughtful attention. Addressing the risks of VR addiction and potential impacts on mental health is crucial to ensuring that individuals can benefit from the immersive experiences without sacrificing real-world interactions. Striking a balance between the virtual and the real is essential for maintaining emotional well-being and social connectedness in an increasingly digitized world. By raising awareness, implementing responsible usage guidelines, and conducting further research, society can embrace the transformative potential of VR while safeguarding the mental health and social fabric of its users.

B. Privacy and Security in Virtual Environments:

As Virtual Reality (VR) technology expands its presence in our lives, the ethical and social considerations surrounding privacy and security become paramount. VR environments raise concerns about data protection, user privacy, and the ethical implications of virtual interactions and identity. In this section, we will delve into the challenges of ensuring data protection in VR, the ethical dimensions of virtual interactions, and the imperative to safeguard user privacy and security in immersive virtual spaces.

Data Protection and User Privacy Concerns:

VR experiences often require users to create accounts and share personal information to access content or engage with other users. As users immerse themselves in virtual environments, their behaviors, interactions, and preferences may be tracked and stored as data. This data holds significant value to VR companies and developers for enhancing user experiences and marketing purposes. However, it also raises concerns about data protection and user privacy.

One primary concern is the potential for data breaches, where sensitive user information could be compromised. In virtual environments, users may interact with others, share personal details, or engage in activities they consider private. VR companies must take robust measures to secure user data, preventing unauthorized access and protecting users from potential harm resulting from data leaks.

Furthermore, concerns exist about how VR companies handle user data and whether it is shared with third parties for marketing or advertising purposes. Transparency in data collection and clear privacy policies are essential to inform users about how their data is used and empower them to make informed decisions about their digital footprint.

Ethical Implications of Virtual Interactions and Identity:

Virtual interactions raise ethical considerations, as they may blur the lines between real-life behaviors and virtual actions. In VR social platforms, users can engage with others through avatars and pseudonyms, leading to a dissociation between actions in the virtual world and their real-world identity.

The anonymity provided by VR environments can lead to unethical behaviors, such as cyberbullying or harassment. The sense of detachment from one's real identity may embolden individuals to engage in actions they would not typically exhibit in face-to-face interactions.

Moreover, VR allows for customization of avatars and personas, giving users the freedom to present themselves as they choose. While this personalization can be empowering, it also raises concerns about authenticity and deception. Virtual interactions may lead to relationships based on false pretenses, potentially leading to emotional harm and trust issues.

Additionally, the potential for virtual identity theft is a new ethical dilemma. As VR environments become more interconnected and support cross-platform experiences, there is a risk of malicious actors assuming other users' identities, leading to potential misuse and fraud.

To address these ethical implications, VR platforms should implement strict policies against harassment and cyberbullying. Ensuring users can report and block abusive behaviors is vital to fostering a safe and inclusive virtual community.

Virtual environments should also provide tools for identity verification, allowing users to confirm their real-world identities voluntarily. This feature can help establish a higher level of trust among users and reduce the likelihood of deception.

Educational programs and awareness campaigns can promote responsible and ethical behavior in virtual interactions. Educating users about the impact of their actions on others, even in virtual settings, can promote empathy and encourage respectful behavior.

In conclusion, as VR becomes an integral part of our digital landscape, addressing privacy, security, and ethical considerations is essential for building a responsible and trustworthy virtual ecosystem. Data protection and user privacy must be prioritized to safeguard users' personal information and preserve their autonomy in virtual environments. The ethical implications of virtual interactions and identity necessitate a thoughtful approach to maintain a positive and respectful virtual community. By implementing robust data protection measures, promoting ethical behavior, and fostering transparency, VR companies can create immersive and secure virtual spaces that enhance user experiences while respecting their rights and values.

CHAPTER VII
The Future of Virtual Reality

A. Emerging Technologies and Possibilities:

Virtual Reality (VR) has already made a significant impact on various industries and aspects of our lives. However, the future of VR promises even more exciting developments, with emerging technologies opening up new possibilities. In this section, we will explore the advancements in augmented reality (AR) and mixed reality (MR), as well as the innovative directions VR is taking beyond visual and auditory experiences.

Augmented Reality and Mixed Reality Developments:

Augmented Reality and Mixed Reality are extensions of VR that blend virtual elements with the real world, enhancing our perception and interaction with the environment.

a. Augmented Reality (AR): AR overlays digital information onto the real world, allowing users to see and interact with virtual objects within their physical surroundings. Smartphones and wearable devices are already leveraging AR technology for applications like navigation, gaming, and advertising. In the future, AR could revolutionize fields like architecture, design, and education, allowing users to visualize and manipulate virtual models in real-world spaces. Medical professionals might use AR to overlay patient data during surgeries, improving precision and decision-making.

b. Mixed Reality (MR): MR takes AR a step further by seamlessly integrating virtual content with the real world, creating a unified experience where physical and digital elements coexist. Advanced MR headsets can map the environment accurately, enabling virtual objects to interact realistically with real-world surfaces and objects. This opens the door to more immersive gaming experiences, collaborative workspaces, and interactive storytelling. In the future, MR could redefine social interactions, allowing people to meet and communicate in virtual spaces while still being aware of their physical surroundings.

VR Innovations Beyond Visual and Auditory Experiences:

While VR has predominantly focused on visual and auditory immersion, the future of VR is set to expand its capabilities to encompass other senses and even haptic feedback.

a. Haptic Feedback: Haptic technology simulates the sense of touch by providing tactile sensations to users. VR systems are already incorporating basic haptic feedback through handheld controllers, but future developments may introduce more sophisticated haptic suits or gloves that offer a wider range of sensations. This would enable users to feel the texture of virtual objects, experience different temperatures, and even perceive pressure and resistance during interactions.

b. Olfactory Sensations: Research is ongoing to introduce olfactory (smell) experiences to VR. Adding realistic scents to virtual environments could significantly enhance immersion and emotional impact. For example, in educational VR simulations, the ability to smell a specific environment (e.g., a forest, historical setting, or medical scenario) could deepen the learning experience.

c. Taste Sensations: Although challenging, some experiments are exploring the integration of taste sensations into VR experiences. The ability to simulate taste could find applications in culinary training, entertainment, or even medical contexts, such as helping patients overcome taste aversions.

d. Full-Body Immersion: The future of VR involves further advancements in full-body immersion. This could entail advanced motion capture systems that translate real-life movements into virtual avatars, allowing users to embody characters and interact in virtual environments more naturally. Combined with haptic feedback and real-time rendering, full-body immersion could lead to a level of presence and interactivity that blurs the lines between the virtual and physical worlds.

e. Brain-Computer Interfaces (BCIs): BCIs hold the potential to revolutionize VR by allowing direct communication between the brain and the virtual environment. As BCIs become more sophisticated and accessible, users could control virtual experiences through their thoughts, opening up a whole new realm of possibilities for VR applications, especially in the fields of accessibility and rehabilitation.

In conclusion, the future of Virtual Reality is an exhilarating landscape of emerging technologies and possibilities. Augmented Reality and Mixed Reality will further bridge the gap between the real and virtual worlds, enhancing our daily experiences and professional pursuits. Beyond the visual and auditory experiences we currently enjoy, VR is heading towards integrating haptic feedback, olfactory sensations, and even taste, creating a multi-sensory immersion that mirrors the complexity of our real-world experiences. Advancements in full-body immersion and brain-computer interfaces will push the boundaries of presence and interaction, transforming the way we interact with virtual content. As technology continues to evolve, the future of VR holds the potential to reshape industries, redefine human-computer interactions, and enrich our lives in ways we can only imagine today.

B. Integrating VR into Society:

The future of Virtual Reality (VR) holds immense promise as this transformative technology continues to advance. As VR becomes more accessible and sophisticated, it is expected to integrate into various aspects of society, revolutionizing industries and reshaping human experiences. In this section, we will explore the potential impact of VR on various industries and anticipate the challenges that lie ahead on the road to widespread integration.

VR's Potential Impact on Various Industries:

a. Entertainment and Media: VR is already making waves in the entertainment industry, enhancing gaming experiences and immersive storytelling. In the future, VR is expected to redefine how we consume content, from movies and TV shows to live events and concerts. VR theaters and immersive theme parks could become commonplace, offering audiences unparalleled entertainment experiences.

b. Education and Training: VR's potential in education and training is vast. Virtual classrooms, interactive learning modules, and realistic simulations are expected to become integral parts of educational institutions. VR will enable learners to explore historical events, distant locations, and complex scientific concepts in ways that traditional methods cannot match. Moreover, industries like healthcare, aviation, and manufacturing will continue to rely on VR for advanced skills training and professional development.

c. Healthcare and Therapy: The integration of VR in healthcare will lead to more effective patient care and therapy. Virtual environments will be used for pain management, physical rehabilitation, and mental health treatment. The ability to simulate medical procedures and anatomical models will improve medical education and enhance surgical training, leading to better outcomes for patients.

d. Architecture and Design: VR's impact on architecture and design will be transformative. Architects can immerse clients in virtual representations of buildings and spaces, allowing them to experience designs before they are constructed. VR will streamline the design process, facilitate collaborative work, and lead to more efficient and sustainable buildings.

e. Tourism and Travel: VR will disrupt the tourism industry, enabling travelers to explore destinations virtually before planning trips. Virtual tours of landmarks, historical sites, and exotic locations will inspire wanderlust and help travelers make informed decisions. Moreover, VR travel experiences will be accessible to those with physical limitations, fostering inclusivity in tourism.

Anticipated Challenges and the Road Ahead:

a. Accessibility and Affordability: While VR technology is advancing rapidly, ensuring accessibility and affordability remains a challenge. High-quality VR hardware can be costly, limiting access for some individuals and communities. The industry must strive to make VR more accessible and inclusive to ensure widespread adoption.

b. Ethical and Legal Considerations: As VR becomes more immersive and realistic, ethical and legal questions will arise. Issues such as virtual property rights, data privacy, and the potential for misuse must be addressed to establish a framework for responsible VR usage.

c. Health and Safety Concerns: Extended VR usage can lead to physical discomfort, eye strain, and motion sickness for some users. Developers must prioritize user comfort and safety, implementing design practices that reduce the risk of adverse effects.

d. Content Quality and Regulation: As the VR content library expands, ensuring content quality and age-appropriate experiences becomes crucial. Age-appropriate content filtering and appropriate regulation will be essential to protect younger users and maintain public trust in VR platforms.

e. Digital Addiction: The immersive nature of VR experiences may lead to concerns about digital addiction. Striking a balance between virtual engagement and real-world interactions is vital to promoting healthy and well-rounded lifestyles.

f. Standardization and Interoperability: The VR industry must work towards standardizing hardware and software to ensure interoperability and ease of use across different devices and platforms. This will encourage developers to create content that can reach a broader audience.

In conclusion, the future integration of Virtual Reality into society holds immense potential to transform industries and human experiences. From entertainment and education to healthcare and architecture, VR's impact will be far-reaching. However, this journey is not without its challenges. Ensuring accessibility, addressing ethical concerns, prioritizing user safety, and maintaining content quality will be crucial to shaping a responsible and sustainable future for VR. By navigating these challenges and leveraging the transformative power of VR, we can unlock a future where immersive experiences enrich our lives, foster creativity, and pave the way for unprecedented possibilities.

Conclusion

A. Reflections on the Journey:

The evolution of Virtual Reality (VR) from its early beginnings to its current state has been nothing short of extraordinary. The journey of VR has taken us on a rollercoaster ride of technological advancements, creative innovations, and transformative applications. As we reflect on this captivating journey, it becomes evident that VR has profoundly impacted numerous aspects of our lives and society as a whole.

From the birth of VR technology in the 1960s and its early experiments to the development of more accessible and immersive VR headsets in recent years, the progress has been remarkable. VR's allure and potential became evident with promises of transforming how we learn, entertain, communicate, and experience the world around us.

The foundations of VR, from understanding the technology and human-computer interaction to exploring its applications in gaming, storytelling, education, and healthcare, opened new frontiers of possibilities. The allure of virtual experiences and the potential for immersive entertainment and education captivated our imaginations, paving the way for VR to become an integral part of various industries.

In the realm of entertainment, VR gaming experiences brought players into fantastical worlds, blurring the line between reality and fiction. VR storytelling and cinematic experiences challenged traditional narrative structures, immersing audiences in interactive and emotionally impactful narratives.

VR's integration into education and training fostered immersive learning environments, allowing students and professionals to practice in realistic and risk-free settings. Medical training, skills development, and therapeutic interventions found new dimensions of effectiveness through VR.

As VR became more pervasive, we confronted ethical and social considerations, including privacy and security, mental health risks, and the responsible use of technology. We recognized the importance of balancing virtual experiences with real-world interactions, ensuring that VR enhances our lives without isolating us from genuine human connections.

As we look to the future, emerging technologies such as augmented reality and mixed reality promise to take VR to even greater heights. Haptic feedback, olfactory sensations, and taste simulations are poised to make virtual experiences even more immersive and engaging. Full-body immersion and brain-computer interfaces may enable us to interact with virtual worlds through our thoughts and physical actions, breaking the barriers between the digital and the physical.

However, the journey ahead is not without its challenges. We must address issues of accessibility, affordability, data protection, ethical considerations, and potential health impacts. Standardization and content regulation will be necessary to foster a responsible and sustainable VR ecosystem that benefits all users.

In conclusion, the journey of Virtual Reality has been a testament to human ingenuity and our relentless pursuit of innovation. From pixels to reality, VR has transformed how we perceive and interact with the world. As we move forward, it is essential to embrace the potential of VR while being mindful of the ethical, social, and technological challenges that lie ahead. By responsibly harnessing the power of VR, we can create a future where immersive experiences enrich our lives, inspire our creativity, and open new frontiers of knowledge and understanding. The journey of VR is an ongoing adventure, and the possibilities it holds are limited only by the bounds of our imagination.

B. The Transformative Power of VR:

The journey through the evolution of Virtual Reality (VR) has unveiled the transformative power of this groundbreaking technology. From its early days as a concept to its current state of widespread adoption, VR has revolutionized industries, reshaped human experiences, and redefined the boundaries of human-computer interaction. The transformative impact of VR is undeniable, as it continues to inspire innovation and shape the future of how we live, learn, and connect with one another.

At its core, VR holds the potential to transport us to new worlds and unlock experiences that were once limited to our imagination. It transcends the constraints of physical reality, allowing us to explore distant lands, traverse time and space, and connect with people across the globe in ways that were previously unimaginable. This power of immersion and presence empowers us to empathize with others, understand different perspectives, and forge meaningful connections.

In the realm of entertainment, VR has elevated gaming experiences to unprecedented levels of realism and interactivity. Gamers find themselves fully immersed in virtual worlds, becoming active participants in the stories they unravel. The entertainment industry has embraced VR as a powerful medium for storytelling, giving rise to innovative narratives that blur the boundaries between reality and fiction.

VR's impact extends far beyond entertainment, as it revolutionizes education and training. Learners can now step into historical events, explore scientific phenomena, and engage in interactive lessons that facilitate deeper understanding and retention. VR has become a catalyst for transformation in medical education, where students and practitioners can hone their skills in virtual surgical simulations and medical scenarios.

Moreover, VR has found its place in therapeutic settings, offering new avenues for mental health treatment, pain management, and rehabilitation. Patients can confront fears through exposure therapy, find solace in calming virtual environments, and participate in physical therapy exercises in a safe and controlled space. The power of VR to heal and empower individuals facing various health challenges is nothing short of extraordinary.

In the corporate world, VR is reshaping how professionals collaborate, innovate, and conduct business. Virtual meetings and remote collaborations have become routine, breaking down geographical barriers and fostering global connectivity. Companies embrace VR for training employees, enhancing team-building exercises, and streamlining design and prototyping processes.

The transformative power of VR extends beyond its current capabilities, as emerging technologies promise even more exciting possibilities. Augmented Reality and Mixed Reality will intertwine virtual and physical realities, while haptic feedback and full-body immersion will deepen the sense of presence. The integration of brain-computer interfaces will redefine how we interact with digital content and usher in an era of direct mind-to-machine communication.

However, harnessing the transformative power of VR requires responsible development, thoughtful regulation, and ethical considerations. Ensuring accessibility, data privacy, and user safety are essential to creating a sustainable and inclusive VR ecosystem. Balancing virtual experiences with real-world interactions remains crucial in preserving genuine human connections.

In conclusion, the transformative power of Virtual Reality is a testament to human creativity and innovation. VR has transcended pixels to become an integral part of our reality, enriching our lives, enhancing our capabilities, and propelling us into the future. The journey of VR continues, and as we navigate the challenges and embrace the possibilities, we hold the keys to a future where the boundaries of what is possible are limited only by the depths of our imagination. The transformative journey of VR has just begun, and the potential it holds for the world is both awe-inspiring and boundless.

C. Looking Forward: The Next Frontier of Virtual Reality

As we conclude our exploration of the evolution and transformative power of Virtual Reality (VR), it becomes evident that this captivating journey is far from over. VR has already made significant strides in reshaping industries and human experiences, but the future promises an exciting new frontier that will propel this technology to even greater heights. Looking forward, the next frontier of VR holds immense potential to revolutionize how we perceive and interact with the world.

One of the most promising aspects of the next frontier of VR is the convergence of technologies. Augmented Reality (AR) and Mixed Reality (MR) are poised to blend seamlessly with VR, creating a unified reality spectrum that bridges the gap between the physical and digital realms. This convergence will result in a truly immersive experience, where virtual elements interact with the real world in unprecedented ways. Imagine a world where virtual objects seamlessly integrate into our daily lives, enhancing our understanding, productivity, and entertainment.

Haptic feedback, a technology that simulates touch and sensation, will continue to advance, providing users with a more tangible and immersive experience. From feeling the texture of virtual objects to experiencing the warmth of sunlight in a virtual environment, haptic feedback will add a new dimension to VR interactions, making virtual experiences feel more real than ever before.

The integration of olfactory and taste sensations into VR experiences holds the potential to further enhance immersion. Imagine walking through a virtual marketplace, smelling the aroma of spices, and tasting exotic dishes as you explore different cultures and cuisines. These multi-sensory experiences will deepen our connection to virtual content and evoke emotions on a whole new level.

Full-body immersion and advanced motion capture will allow us to embody avatars and interact with virtual worlds using natural movements. As we gesture and move, our virtual counterparts will mimic our actions, creating a sense of presence and agency that blurs the line between ourselves and our digital personas.

Brain-Computer Interfaces (BCIs) represent a revolutionary step in VR technology. By directly communicating with our brains, BCIs will enable us to control virtual environments and interact with digital content through our thoughts. This level of direct neural interface will open doors to new forms of communication, expression, and creativity.

Furthermore, VR's integration with artificial intelligence and machine learning will lead to personalized and adaptive experiences. VR environments will learn from users' preferences and behaviors, tailoring content to individual needs and preferences. This dynamic adaptation will make VR experiences more engaging and relevant to each user.

The next frontier of VR will also be characterized by greater accessibility and inclusivity. Advances in hardware and software will make VR more affordable and user-friendly, allowing a broader audience to participate in its immersive experiences. VR will find applications in fields we have yet to fully explore, such as architecture, urban planning, and scientific research.

As we embrace this next frontier, we must remain mindful of the ethical considerations that come with such powerful technology. Responsible development, data privacy, content regulation, and maintaining genuine human connections will be vital in shaping a future where VR enriches our lives without overshadowing our physical reality.

In conclusion, the next frontier of Virtual Reality is a realm of boundless possibilities. The convergence of technologies, multi-sensory experiences, full-body immersion, and brain-computer interfaces will redefine human experiences and how we interact with digital content. As we venture into this new era, our imagination is the only limit to what VR can achieve. With responsible innovation and a commitment to creating a positive and inclusive VR ecosystem, we stand on the cusp of a transformative revolution that will shape our world in ways we can only begin to imagine. The journey of Virtual Reality continues, and the path ahead is illuminated by the endless possibilities it holds for the future.